THE VOYAGER FAMILY

THE VOYAGER FAMILY

Fred Kerr

PEN & SWORD
TRANSPORT

First published in Great Britain in 2018 by
Pen & Sword Transport
An imprint of
Pen & Sword Books Ltd
47 Church Street
Barnsley
South Yorkshire
S70 2AS

Copyright © Fred Kerr 2018

ISBN 978 1 52673 144 9

A CIP catalogue record for this book is
available from the British Library.

Typeset in 11pt Minion by Mac Style
Printed and bound in India by Replika Press Pvt Ltd

Pen & Sword Books Limited incorporates the imprints of Atlas, Archaeology, Aviation, Discovery, Family History,
Fiction, History, Maritime, Military, Military Classics, Politics, Select, Transport, True Crime, Air World,
Frontline Publishing, Leo Cooper, Remember When, Seaforth Publishing, The Praetorian Press,
Wharncliffe Local History, Wharncliffe Transport, Wharncliffe True Crime and White Owl.

For a complete list of Pen & Sword titles please contact
PEN & SWORD BOOKS LIMITED
47 Church Street, Barnsley, South Yorkshire, S70 2AS, England
E-mail: enquiries@pen-and-sword.co.uk
Website: www.pen-and-sword.co.uk

Front Cover: Class 220 220015 *Solway Voyager* awaits departure from Edinburgh Waverley on 10 November 2004 with a service to Aberdeen.

Rear Cover: Class 220 'Voyager' trainset 220004 *Cumbrian Voyager* descends through Greenholme on 6 April 2007 whilst working a southbound Cross Country service.

Contents

In 1996 Virgin Trains was awarded the Inter City Cross Country franchise to run from 5 January 1997 until November 2007. When the franchise began, its services were operated by a mix of traction including ailing Class 47 diesel locomotives traversing non-electrified routes and ageing Class 86 electric locomotives travsersing electrified routes.

As part of the franchise agreement, the Cross Country services called for a fleet of new trainsets, resulting in the ordering of thirty-four 4-car trainsets designated Class 220 and forty 5-car + four 4-car trainsets with tilt mechanism for 125 mph operation designated Class 221; classified as 'Voyager' and 'Super Voyager' respectively these were ordered from Bombardier Transportation which built them at its Bruges factory in Belgium.

The new trainsets began to be delivered from mid-2001 and, once driver and artisan training had been completed, they began to replace the current mix of locomotives to provide a more standard fleet. The timetable was also rewritten and, under the title of 'Operation Princess', Virgin Trains launched it in September 2002 based on clock-face schedules with shorter trains but more frequent services. The new timetable, however, proved to be too optimistic and a combination of technical faults with the trainsets, coupled with infrastructure and train capacity problems, led to the cutting of less-used services during 2003 in order to maintain the main services at a higher level of reliability.

In 2006 the Department for Transport (DfT) decided to restructure the Virgin Trains franchises and create a revised one for Cross Country services; although Virgin Trains was one of the contenders for this, the DfT awarded the franchise to Arriva Trains on 10 July 2007 with a start date of 11 November 2007. As part of the takeover the Class 220 fleet and twenty-three Class 221 trainsets were transferred to the new operator where they remain in service as at June 2017.

The next purchaser of 'Voyager trainsets' was Midland Mainline, owned by National Express, whose franchise ran from April 1996 to November 2007 covering services from London St Pancras. In February 2002 the company sought to extend services to Leeds and ordered seven 9-car and sixteen 4-car trainsets based on the 'Voyager' design; designated Class 222 the company classified them as 'Meridian' but design changes meant that the 'Meridian' trainsets could not couple up to the 'Voyager' trainsets. The Strategic Rail Authority (SRA), however, subsequently refused to allow the proposed service extensions or sanction the operation of the 9-car trainsets thus delaying their introduction into traffic until 31 May 2004.

The increase in traffic, however, saw the units being reformed in 2006 and they were initially retained by Stagecoach Group, trading as East Midland Trains (EMT), when it took over the franchise in November 2007. Shortly after the takeover EMT reconfigured the trainsets once more and the fleet still operates in this form as at June 2017.

The final purchaser of 'Voyager' trainsets design was Hull Trains (HT), an Open Access operator which began operations in December 2000 to provide a service between Hull and London Kings Cross. Traffic increased quickly and the company ordered four 4-car 'Meridian' trainsets that were classified Class 222.1 and designated as 'Pioneer' when they entered service in 2005. The four trainsets were subsequently transferred to EMT in 2009 when HT arranged to lease surplus Class 180 trainsets to meet the increasing demand for its services.

Fred Kerr
November 2017

A Class 220 trainset curves out of Newcastle on 12 March 2004 with a northbound Cross Country service to Edinburgh.

Section 1:
Class 220 'Voyager'

1.1: Virgin Trains

The thirty-four Class 220 'Voyager' trainsets were ordered by Virgin Trains as part of the franchise agreement and formed part of an order that included the Class 221 'Super Voyager' trainsets [see **Section 2**] and Class 390 'Pendelino' tilting trainsets to replace the mix of trainsets operating services on the West Coast Main Line (WCML). The Cross Country services were operated by a mix of traction including Class 43 HST trainsets, Class 47 diesel locomotives and Classes 86, 87 and 90 electric locomotives with some journeys being worked by diesel traction throughout, some with changes between diesel and electric traction en route and some with electric traction throughout. The majority of Cross Country's longer distance services involving locomotive changes en route or using Class 47 locomotives were the first services for which the Class 220 trainsets entered traffic as direct replacements. The 'Voyager' order was set to speed up services by eliminating traction changes en route whilst improving efficiency by operating a standard fleet; the trainsets were built by Bombardier at their Bruges factory in Belgium and deliveries began during 2001. As part of the contract the trainsets were maintained at a dedicated site at Central Rivers (Barton under Needwood) by Bombardier; this continued when the Cross Country franchise was awarded to Arriva Trains in November 2007 and still operates as at June 2017.

In September 2002 Virgin Trains rolled out a new timetable for its 'Voyager' fleet under the title of Operation Princess which set Birmingham New St as a hub through which services were operated to a clock-face timetable using shorter trainsets on more frequent services. The scheme failed because of both technical problems with the trainsets and operating problems with the infrastructure that resulted in some services being withdrawn during 2003 to protect the core services – especially the longer distance ones.

In 2006 the Department for Transport decided to restructure the Virgin franchises and create a revised one for Cross Country services. Although Virgin Trains was one of the contenders, the Department for Transport (DfT) awarded the franchise to Arriva Trains on 10 July 2007 with a start date of 11 November 2007; as part of the takeover the Class 220 fleet was transferred to the new operator and re-liveried.

220004 *Cumbrian Voyager* eases out of Ribblehead on 24 January 2004 whilst working a Birmingham New St–Edinburgh service that had been diverted from the WCML due to engineering works between Preston and Carlisle.

The initial range of services included a Portsmouth–Blackpool North working which then ran to Preston for overnight servicing. On 29 March 2002 220022 *Brighton Voyager* and 220011 *Tyne Voyager* stand in Preston as they receive the attention of cleaning and maintenance staff.

The introduction of the 'Voyager' trainsets obviated the need for locomotive changes at Preston for services operated to Blackpool or operated via Manchester Piccadilly hence the Preston area became an early location to see the new trainsets at work.

220017 *Bombardier Voyager* + 220015 *Solway Voyager* race through Leyland on 26 February 2002 with an Edinburgh–Brighton service running via Manchester Piccadilly.

220013 *Gwibiwr de Cymru/South Wales Voyager* curves through the approach to Chorley on 18 October 2003 whilst en route to Manchester Piccadilly with a southbound Cross Country service.

220019 *Mersey Voyager* calls at Preston on 29 January 2007 whilst working a Plymouth–Aberdeen service.

220021 *Staffordshire Voyager* calls at Bolton on 24 January 2007 whilst working an Edinburgh–Manchester Piccadilly service.

Right: 220004 *Cumbrian Voyager* races through Greenholme on 4 April 2007 with a southbound Cross Country service.

Below: 220025 *Severn Voyager* stands at Blackpool North on 18 February 2003 awaiting departure for Birmingham International.

220010 *Ribble Voyager* races through Brock on 22 April 2004 as it nears Preston with a southbound Cross Country service.

220003 *Solent Voyager* curves through Lancaster on 26 January 2005 with an Edinburgh–Manchester Piccadilly service.

220006 *Clyde Voyager* curves into Lancaster on 2 November 2006 whilst working a southbound Cross Country service.

220002 *Forth Voyager* curves through Oubeck after leaving Lancaster on 2 November 2006 whilst working a Glasgow Central–Plymouth service.

An unidentified 'Voyager' trainset races through Brock on 12 May 2006 as it nears Preston with a southbound Cross Country service.

220002 *Forth Voyager* climbs through Greenholme on 28 July 2006 with a northbound Cross Country service.

Left: 220001 *Somerset Voyager* passes Docker on 22 March 2005 with a southbound Cross Country service.

Right: 220016 *Midland Voyager* curves through Beckfoot on 20 October 2003 with a Birmingham New St–Glasgow Central service.

Left: 220011 *Tyne Voyager* curves through Beckfoot on 4 April 2007 with a southbound Cross Country service.

220024 *Sheffield Voyager* climbs through Greenholme on 18 April 2007 with a northbound Cross Country service.

Above: 220023 *Mancunian Voyager* passes the outskirts of Clitheroe on 14 April 2007 with an Exeter Central–Glasgow Central service diverted from its normal WCML route due to engineering works between Preston and Carlisle.

Below: 220026 *Stagecoach Voyager* + Class 221 221138 *Thor Heyerdahl* curve past Langcliffe on 14 April 2007 with a Glasgow Central–Plymouth service diverted from its normal WCML route due to engineering works between Preston and Carlisle.

220009 *Gatwick Voyager* + Class 221 221110 *James Cook* climb past Billington on 31 March 2007 with a Glasgow Central–Plymouth service diverted from its normal WCML route due to engineering works between Preston and Carlisle.

Above: 220028 *Black Country Voyager* + 220005 *Guildford Voyager* approach the Warrington Bank Quay stop of their Glasgow Central–Paignton service on 31 May 2003.

Left: 220008 *Draig Gymreig/Welsh Dragon* is refuelled at Longsight Depot on 17 May 2005 during its overnight stay for servicing and maintenance.

Below: 220004 *Cumbrian Voyager* awaits departure from Preston on 11 March 2003 with a Birmingham International–Blackpool North service.

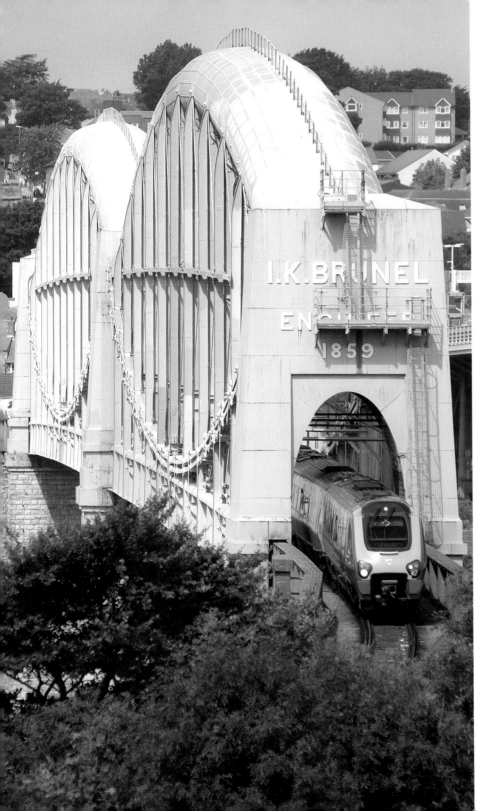

Above: 220004 *Cumbrian Voyager* + Class 221 221143 *Auguste Picard* skirt the sea wall at Dawlish on 27 April 2004 whilst working a Penzance–Dundee service.

Left: 220022 *Brighton Voyager* enters Devon as it curves off the Tamar Bridge on 20 July 2005 whilst working a Penzance–Glasgow Central service.

Below: 220033 *Fife Voyager* + Class 221 221108 *Sir Ernest Shackleton* power through Dawlish on 25 October 2004 whilst working a Penzance–Dundee service.

A brief respite at Rattery Bank on 27 November 2004 sees the passing of Edinburgh–Plymouth services with (*Left*) a 'Voyager' trainset heading north to Edinburgh whilst (*Right*) another 'Voyager' trainset nears journey's end at Plymouth.

A 'Voyager' trainset speeds through Acton Bridge on 5 April 2006 shortly after leaving Warrington Bank Quay with a southbound Cross Country service.

Scenes from Winwick, on the northern outskirts of Warrington

220012 *Lanarkshire Voyager* powers a southbound Cross Country service on 22 March 2006.

220007 *Thames Voyager* heads north on 7 December 2004 with a Plymouth–Edinburgh service.

220020 *Wessex Voyager* heads north on 18 June 2004 with a Bristol–Glasgow Central service.

220029 *Vyajer Kernewek/Cornish Voyager* heads north on 24 March 2004 with a Plymouth–Glasgow Central service.

220014 *South Yorkshire Voyager* heads south of Crewe on 26 September 2004 with a southbound Cross Country service.

220005 *Guildford Voyager* passes Fenwick on 14 July 2006 en route to York with a northbound Cross Country service.

220027 *Avon Voyager* curves through Edinburgh's Princes St Gardens on 11 February 2003 with a Dundee–Cardiff service.

220034 *Yorkshire Voyager* prepares to depart from Alnmouth on 11 March 2004 with an Edinburgh–Bristol service.

220015 *Solway Voyager* + 220013 *Gwibiwr de Cymru/South Wales Voyager* curve through Portway on 29 September 2003 as they near Tamworth with a southbound Cross County service.

220018 *Dorset Voyager* curves through Culham on 26 April 2004 with a southbound Cross Country service.

220032 *Grampian Voyager* curves through Euxton on 5 May 2003 with a southbound Cross Country service.

...yager curves through Norton Bridge on 26 September 2004 as it joins the WCML with a Macclesfield–Birmingham New St service.

220015 *Solway Voyager* waits under the shadow of Edinburgh Castle on 10 November 2004 to depart with a service to Aberdeen.

220016 *Midland Voyager* curves through Clay Cross on 9 November 2007 with a southbound Cross Country service.

220025 *Severn Voyager* performs a stock move at Bristol Temple Meads on 8 June 2004 prior to returning north with a Cross Country service.

220027 *Avon Voyager* + Class 221 221112 *Ferdinand Magellan* curve through Beckfoot on 22 April 2005 whilst working a Glasgow Central–Penzance service.

Right: 220033 *Fife Voyager* curves through Greenholme on 28 January 2004 as its ascends Shap with a Bristol–Glasgow Central service.

Below: A 'Voyager' trainset weaves along the East Coast at Lamberton on 11 March 2004 as it approaches the England/Scotland border whilst working a Leeds–Edinburgh service.

A 'Voyager' trainset curves through Kings Sutton on 10 February 2005 whilst working a northbound Cross Country service.

A 'Voyager' trainset breasts Ais Gill on 17 January 2004 whilst working a Birmingham New St–Edinburgh service diverted to the Settle & Carlisle route from its normal Preston–Carlisle route by engineering works.

1.2: Arriva Trains

The new franchise granted to Arriva Trains, trading as Cross Country Trains, began on 11 November 2007 when drastic changes were made to the Cross Country services and the new company took over the thirty-four Class 220 + twenty-three class 221 trainsets from Virgin Trains, plus a number of Class 170 Turbostar trainsets from Central Trains, to work them. The main difference was that, whilst services still operated through Birmingham as the hub centre, the only West Coast routed services were those that now terminated at Manchester Piccadilly whilst services to centres north of there were operated over the old North East - South West (Newcastle–Bristol) route. All services north of Newcastle thus continued on the ECML leaving the WCML bereft of Cross Country services north of Manchester.

In preparation for the transfer of trainsets all Class 220 trainsets were de-named whilst some lost their Virgin Trains branding and, after the takeover date, some were given temporary Cross Country Trains branding as a prelude to full liveries being applied at a later date.

Trainsets operating without Virgin Trains branding as noted at Clay Cross on 9 November 2007

Below: 220001 *Somerset Voyager* retains its nameplate but has lost its Virgin Trains branding as it heads north on a Cross Country service.

Right: A 'Voyager' trainset with both nameplates and Virgin Trains branding removed heads south with a Cross Country service.

Trainsets operating with Virgin Trains livery and Cross Country branding

Displaying the temporary Cross Country Trains branding, 220023 passes Shipston en route to Newcastle on 29 May 2008 with a northbound Cross Country service.

Scenes of the 'Voyager' trainsets with temporary branding include:

Above: 220013 curving through Colton on 8 May 2008 as it approaches York with a northbound Cross Country service.

Right: 220014 awaiting departure from Manchester Piccadilly on 7 February 2008 with a service to Reading.

Below: 220016 curving into Manchester Piccadilly on 18 April 2008 at the end of its journey from Brighton.

Above: Class doyen 220001 stands in Manchester Piccadilly on 18 April 2008 awaiting departure for Reading.

Right: 220028 races through Copmanthorpe on 27 August 2013 after leaving York with a Newcastle–Southampton service.

Below: 220033 curves through Longbridge on 16 May 2012 whilst working a Newcastle–Bristol service.

220015 approaches Basingstoke on 18 April 2011 whilst working a Bournemouth–Manchester Piccadilly service.

220002 races through Beaulieu Road in the New Forest on 29 May 2009 whilst working a Bournemouth–Manchester Piccadilly service.

220002 races through Copmanthorpe on 7 March 2011 whilst approaching York with a northbound Cross Country service.

39

Above: 220009 curves through Clay Cross on 3 April 2009 whilst working a northbound Cross Country service.

Right: 220014 curves through Kings Sutton on 11 March 2011 whilst working a northbound Cross Country service.

A pair of 'Voyager' trainsets led by 220018 passes Elford whilst en route from Birmingham New St to the Central Rivers depot at Barton under Needwood for maintenance.

A 'Voyager' trainset passes Portway on 26 June 2008 with a northbound Cross Country service.

220019 curves through Kings Sutton on 3 August 2013 whilst working a Bournemouth–Manchester Piccadilly service.

220030 passes Portway on 26 June 2008 with a southbound Cross Country service.

220027 curves through Clay Cross on 3 April 2009 with a southbound Cross Country service.

Section 2:
Class 221 'Super Voyager'

2.1: Virgin Trains

The Class 221 'Super Voyager' trainsets were designed as 5-coach trainsets fitted with tilt equipment and geared for 125 mph operation over both the WCML and ECML portions of their Cross Country services. In the event the first deliveries of these trainsets were as 4-car units with the 5th car being supplied as the final production except for the last four trainsets (221141–44) which remained as 4-car units to work North Wales services from Euston to Holyhead.

When the Cross Country franchise passed to Arriva Trains, the fleet was split between Virgin Trains and Arriva Trains. Virgin retained 221101–221118 + 221142–221144 to work services between Birmingham and Edinburgh/Glasgow which remained in the Virgin Franchise, and to provide trainsets when services were diverted over non-electrified routes. When new services were established to serve Chester and Holyhead the 'Super Voyager' trainsets were also used on these services with the Class 390 Pendelino trainsets re-diagrammed to release them from WCML services. Virgin Trains later de-commissioned trainset 221144 to convert 221142/3 to standard 5-car units and provide two spare driving power cars for training purposes.

Arriva Trains received trainsets 221119–221141 (including the 4-car unit 221141) which received the same treatment as the Class 220 'Voyager' trainsets in respect of names and branding. The initial need to undertake modifications to the sanding equipment on the 'Super Voyager' trainsets saw the company borrow 221114–18 from Virgin Trains for a short period during which time Virgin branding was removed. Arriva subsequently identified reliability problems with the fleet and de-commissioned the tilt unit thus removing the 125 mph capability whilst increasing reliability and making them more compatible with the Class 220 'Voyager' trainsets.

4-car trainset 221104 *Sir John Franklin* + Class 220 220030 *Devon Voyager* curve through Chorley on 9 May 2002 with a Bournemouth–Edinburgh service.

As class doyen, 221101 *Louis Bleriot* was subject to testing by the Research Department at Derby before entering normal service. On 16 November 2002 it was subject to overnight test running between Preston and Carnforth and is noted at Preston in its 4-car formation awaiting its next northbound run.

221119 *Amelia Earhart* curves into Stockport on 17 August 2002 whilst working a Manchester Piccadilly–Stafford crew training service.

A 'Super Voyager' trainset approaches Leyland on 24 April 2002 whilst working an Edinburgh–Brighton service.

Above: A 'Super Voyager' trainset climbs past Greenholme on 4 January 2003 whilst working a Birmingham New St–Edinburgh service.

Right: A 'Super Voyager' trainset curves through Portway on 29 September 2003 whilst working a southbound Cross Country service.

Problems at Preston on 23 November 2002 as 221129 *George Vancouver* (on the left) stands after failing whilst working a Bournemouth–Edinburgh service and 221143 *Auguste Picard* (on the right), working a Penzance–Glasgow Central service, was commandeered to couple up to the failed unit and work the combined trainset forward.

An overnight respite at Longsight depot on 17 November 2005 sees (left) Class 220 220008 *Draig Gymreig/Welsh Dragon* and (right) Class 221 221134 *Mary Kingsley* being refuelled and serviced.

221143 *Auguste Picard* curves through Winwick on 22 March 2006 with a southbound Cross Country service.

221142 *Matthew Flinders* calls at Bolton on 23 January 2007 whilst working an Edinburgh–Manchester Piccadilly service.

221143 *Auguste Picard* + 221109 *Marco Polo* curve through Euxton on 9 July 2009 with a Lancaster–Euston service.

221144 *Prince Madoc* curves through Oubeck on 2 November 2006 with a Birmingham New St–Edinburgh service.

221141 *Amerigo Vespucci* curves through Oubeck on 2 November 2006 with an Edinburgh–Manchester Piccadilly service.

When the split of trainsets between Virgin Trains and Arriva Trains took place in November 2007, Virgin Trains retained 3 4-car Class 221 trainsets 221142–44 but during 2011 Virgin Trains elected to split trainset 221144 to convert 221142/3 to standard 5-car units whilst providing 2 Driving Motor vehicles for spares/training purposes.

In 2017 the 2 Driving Motor vehicles of 221144 were transferred to Arriva Trains, which had removed a Motor Vehicle from two of its 'Super Voyager' trainsets and, in related train reformations involving Virgin Trains trainsets 221142/43, 221144 was restored to a 4-car trainset. This resulted in Arriva Trains operating 4x4-car 'Super Voyager' trainsets numbered 22136/40/41/44 from November 2017.

THE OLD ORDER

Left: 221142 *Matthew Flinders* races through Brock on 5 February 2004 with a Birmingham New St–Edinburgh service.

Below Left: 221144 *Prince Madoc* is the rear of a northbound Cross Country service which curves onto Ribblehead Viaduct on 1 May 2005 when WCML services were diverted over the Settle & Carlisle route due to engineering works on the normal WCML route between Preston and Carlisle.

Below Right: 221143 *Auguste Picard* races past Balshaw Lane on 7 May 2008 whilst working a Birmingham New St–Edinburgh service.

THE NEW ORDER

Once converted to 5-car trainsets the ex 4-car trainsets became indistinguishable from the remainder of the Virgin Trains 5-car fleet.

Right: 221142, now renamed *Bombardier Voyager*, curves through Winwick on 13 January 2012 whilst working a Glasgow Central–Birmingham New St service.

Below Left: The spare Driving Motor vehicles from 221144 Prince Madoc were noted as display items during a visit to the NRM (York) RailFest2012 event on 5 June 2012.

Below Right: 221143 *Auguste Picard* + 221102 *John Cabot* curve through Euxton on 4 December 2013 whilst working an Edinburgh–Birmingham New St service.

Above: The original image, showing a 'Super Voyager' trainset skirting the sea wall at Dawlish on 26 April 2004 with a westbound Cross Country service, is "cropped" to produce the images at left and below.

Above: 221109 *Marco Polo* + 221106 *Willem Barents* are nose-to-nose as they pass Brock on 11 February 2009 whilst working a Lancaster–Euston service.

Right: 221107 *Sir Martin Frobisher* passes Brock on 11 February 2009 whilst working a Glasgow Central–Birmingham New St service.

Below: 221119 *Amelia Earhart* hurries along the WCML at Sytch Lane on 12 August 2003 whilst working a northbound Cross Country service.

The early days of their service found Class 221 trainsets frequently diverted over the Settle & Carlisle route when engineering works took place between Preston and Carlisle; this also routed trains through the Ribble Valley.

Ribble Valley

221112 *Ferdinand Magellan* + 221103 *Christopher Columbus* curve through Clitheroe on 29 March 2008 with a diverted Birmingham New St–Glasgow Central service.

221101 *Louis Bleriot* + 221144 *Prince Madoc* pass through Clitheroe on 29 March 2008 with a diverted Glasgow Central–Birmingham New St service.

A 'Super Voyager' trainset crosses Whalley Viaduct and approaches Whalley station on 29 April 2006 with a diverted Birmingham New St–Carlisle service.

Appleby

221104 *Sir John Franklin* + Class 220 220027 *Avon Voyager* approach Appleby on 26 March 2005 whilst working a diverted Penzance–Glasgow Central service.

221121 *Charles Darwin* + 221122 *Doctor Who* approach Appleby on 26 March 2005 whilst working a diverted Glasgow Central–Penzance service.

Above: 221101 *Louis Bleriot* curves off the Tamar Bridge into Devon on 20 July 2005 whilst working a Penzance–Dundee service.

Right: 221116 *David Livingstone* curves out of Dawlish Warren on 27 April 2004 whilst working a Birmingham New St–Plymouth service.

Below: 221111 *Roald Amundsen* calls at Stockport on 1 November 2003 whilst working a Manchester Piccadilly–Birmingham New St service.

Left: A 'Super Voyager' trainset eases through Norton Bridge on 26 September 2004 as it approaches the WCML with a southbound Cross Country service from Manchester Piccadilly.

Below Left: 221113 *Sir Walter Raleigh* races past Sytch Lane on 12 August 2003 whilst working a southbound Cross Country service.

Below Right: 221101 *Louis Bleriot* curves past Heamies Bridge on 27 March 2012 whilst working a Euston–Chester service.

221117 *Sir Henry Morton Stanley* approaches Deganwy on 27 September 2004 whilst working Virgin Trains' initial Euston–Llandudno service.

221130 *Michael Palin* races past Abergele on 27 September 2004 whilst working a Euston–Holyhead service.

Right: The old scene at Chorley Royal Ordnance Factory sees the site 'recovered' by nature as 221112 *Ferdinand Magellan* passes on 26 August 2004 with a Glasgow Central–Bournemouth service diverted from its normal WCML route by engineering works between Preston and Crewe.

Left: The new station at Buckshaw, named Bucksaw Parkway, was funded by Tesco as part of its planning permission to build a supermarket within the new development and where, on 14 July 2013, a pair of 'Super Voyager' trainsets passed through whilst working a Preston–Birmingham New St service diverted from its normal WCML route by engineering works between Preston and Crewe.

Right: The new scene at Chorley Royal Ordnance Factory, now renamed Buckshaw, sees the site being cleared for housing development as 221107 *Sir Martin Frobisher* + 221113 *Sir Walter Raleigh* pass on 18 July 2013 whilst working a Preston–Birmingham New St service diverted from its normal WCML route by engineering works between Preston and Crewe.

A 'Super Voyager' trainset curves through the approach to Chorley on 18 October 2003 with a southbound Cross Country service.

221122 *Doctor Who* curves out of Chorley on 20 May 2005 with a Bournemouth–Glasgow Central service.

Right: 221102 *John Cabot* races through Brock on 2 February 2013 whilst working a Glasgow Central–Birmingham New St service.

Below Left: 221125 *Henry the Navigator* powers through Brock on 22 April 2004 whilst working a southbound Cross Country service.

Below Right: 221105 *William Baffin* races through Brock on 9 May 2011 whilst working a Birmingham New St–Edinburgh service.

Opposite Page: A 'Super Voyager' trainset races south through Winwick on 26 November 2009 with a Glasgow Central–Birmingham New St service.

221122 *Doctor Who* works a Glasgow Central–Bournemouth service on 17 September 2003.

221115 *Sir Francis Chichester* works a Plymouth–Edinburgh service on 30 December 2002.

221121 *Charles Darwin* works a Plymouth–Edinburgh service on 6 May 2004.

221110 *James Cook* works a northbound Cross Country service on 23 June 2005.

A 'Super Voyager' trainset works a northbound Cross Country service through Leyland on 17 October 2003.

221113 *Sir Walter Raleigh* + 221142 *Matthew Flinders* climb through Euxton on 21 June 2009 with an Edinburgh–Birmingham New St service.

221129 *George Vancouver* climbs through Euxton on 25 May 2007 with a southbound Cross Country service.

Scenes at Balshaw Lane Junction

221108 *Sir Ernest Shackleton* passes on 7 September 2011 with a Birmingham New St–Edinburgh service.

A 'Super Voyager' trainset passes on the 2-track stretch on 26 September 2007 with a northbound Cross Country service.

Above: 221106 *Willem Barents* approaches on 14 April 2016 with a Euston–Birmingham New St–Edinburgh service.

Right: A 'Super Voyager' trainset approaches on 4 May 2011 with a Birmingham New St–Glasgow Central service.

221128 *Captain John Smith* departs with an Edinburgh–Plymouth service on 18 August 2005.

221137 *Mayflower Pilgrims* rests after its arrival with a Bristol–Preston service on 7 September 2002.

Scenes from Greenholme I

A pair of 'Super Voyager' trainsets passes on 28 January 2012 with a Birmingham New St–Edinburgh service.

221127 *Wright Brothers* passes on 3 June 2006 with a northbound Cross Country service.

221125 *Henry the Navigator* passes on 18 April 2007 with a northbound Cross Country service.

221104 *Sir John Franklin* passes on 2 May 2008 with a Birmingham New St–Edinburgh service.

221114 *Sir Francis Drake* passes on 4 January 2003 with a Bristol–Glasgow Central service.

221107 *Sir Martin Frobisher* passes on 4 January 2003 with a Reading–Edinburgh service.

221110 *James Cook* passes on 14 June 2012 with a Birmingham New St–Glasgow Central service.

221138 *Thor Heyerdahl* passes on 18 April 2007 with a northbound Cross Country service.

221103 *Christopher Columbus* powers off Ribblehead Viaduct on 1 May 2005 with a southbound Cross Country working.

221135 *Donald Campbell* passes Ribblehead on 31 January 2004 with an Edinburgh–Plymouth service.

221132 *William Spiers Bruce* eases through Ribblehead on 29 April 2006 with a Plymouth–Carlisle service.

221140 *Vasco da Gamma* + 221142 *Matthew Flinders* pass Selside on 17 January 2004 with a Plymouth–Glasgow Central service.

221137 *Mayflower Pilgrims* + 221105 *William Baffin* curve through Langcliffe on 14 April 2007 with a Plymouth–Glasgow Central service.

A 'Super Voyager' trainset climbs through Greenholme on 30 December 2009 whilst working a Birmingham New St–Glasgow Central service.

221118 *Mungo Park* passes Little Strickland on 17 October 2009 whilst working a Glasgow Central–Birmingham New St service.

Right: A 'Super Voyager' trainset curves through Greenholme on 1 July 2008 whilst working an Edinburgh–Birmingham New St service.

Far Right: A 'Super Voyager' trainset curves through the Lune Gorge on 22 March 2005 whilst working a northbound Cross Country service.

Below: 221136 *Yuri Gagarin* passes Beckfoot on 31 January 2003 with a Glasgow Central–Plymouth service.

Left: 221106 *Willem Barents* curves through the approach to Chorley on 6 March 2005 with a Preston–Plymouth service diverted via Manchester due to engineering works between Preston and Crewe.

Below: 221111 *Roald Amundsen* leaves Lancaster on 26 January 2005 whilst working an Edinburgh–Plymouth service.

221109 *Marco Polo* curves off the WCML at Norton Bridge on 26 September 2004 whilst working a Birmingham New St–Macclesfield service.

221126 *Captain Robert Scott* stands in Preston on 7 September 2002 after its arrival with a terminating service from Bristol.

Right: 221126 *Captain Robert Scott* weaves through Edinburgh's Princes St Gardens on 10 November 2004 whilst working an Edinburgh–Plymouth service.

Below: 221117 *Sir Henry Morton Stanley* approaches Berwick on Tweed on 16 June 2005 whilst working a southbound Cross Country service.

Right: 221107 *Sir Martin Frobisher* eases its Edinburgh–Manchester Piccadilly service through Edinburgh's Princes St Gardens on 10 November 2004.

Below: A 'Super Voyager' trainset stands in Edinburgh Waverley on 7 April 2005 awaiting the signal to depart to Craigentinny CS for overnight servicing.

Scenes at Winwick

221115 *Polmadie Depot* curves through on 19 May 2011 whilst working a Glasgow Central–Birmingham New St service.

221134 *Mary Kingsley* curves through on 7 December 2004 whilst working an Edinburgh–Plymouth service.

221124 *Charles Lindbergh* curves through on 18 December 2002 whilst working an Edinburgh–Plymouth service.

A 'Super Voyager' trainset curves through on 13 May 2008 whilst working an Edinburgh–Birmingham New St service.

Scenes at Acton Bridge

Right: A 'Super Voyager' trainset approaches on 12 May 2005 whilst working a southbound Cross Country service.

Bottom Right: A 'Super Voyager' trainset approaches on 5 April 2006 whilst working a southbound Cross Country service.

Bottom Left: 221118 *Mungo Park* approaches on 12 May 2005 whilst working a southbound Cross Country service.

Above: A 'Super Voyager' trainset curves through Clay Cross on 7 May 2005 whilst working a southbound Cross Country service.

Right: A 'Super Voyager' trainset races up the ECML at Fenwick on 14 July 2006 with a northbound Cross Country service.

Below: A 'Super Voyager' trainset curves through Winwick on 20 March 2007 whilst working a northbound Cross Country service.

Top Left: 221106 *Willem Barents* climbs out of Llandudno Junction on 24 April 2010 whilst working a Holyhead–Euston service.

Top Right: A 'Super Voyager' trainset curves away from Kings Sutton on 10 February 2005 whilst working a northbound Cross Country service.

Below: A 'Super Voyager' trainset races past Burnmouth on 10 March 2004 whilst working an Edinburgh–Bristol service.

221123 *Henry Hudson* drifts past Tupton on 5 July 2006 whilst working a northbound Cross Country service.

221139 *Leif Erikson* curves through Oubeck on 3 June 2006 whilst working a Birmingham New St–Glasgow Central service.

221138 *Thor Heyerdahl* climbs the approach to Chorley on 3 October 2004 with an Edinburgh–Oxford service diverted via Manchester due to engineering work on the normal WCML Preston–Crewe route.

221133 *Alexander Selkirk* drifts past Tupton on 5 July 2006 whilst working a southbound Cross Country service.

221128 *Captain John Smith* curves through Morpeth on 11 March 2004 with a Bristol–Edinburgh service.

221140 *Vasco da Gama* + Class 220 220018 *Dorset Voyager* pass Coed Kernow on 29 February 2004 whilst working a Cardiff–Bristol shuttle service run in conjunction with a Rugby International game being held at Cardiff's Millennium Stadium.

Right: 221131 *Edgar Evans* performs a station shunt move at Bristol Temple Meads on 8 June 2004 prior to returning north with a Cross Country service.

Below: 221127 *Wright Brothers* stands at the Glasgow Central buffers on 7 April 2005 awaiting departure with a southbound Cross Country service.

2.2: Arriva Trains

When Arriva Trains took over the Cross Country franchise and the Class 220 'Voyager'/221 'Super Voyager' trainsets in November 2007, there was an interim period when trainsets were operated either without branding (see also page 34) or with temporary Cross Country branding (see also pages 35–6). Examples of these temporary liveries as applied to the 'Super Voyager' trainsets are noted below.

Trainsets operating without Virgin Trains branding

Top Left: 221114 climbs through Leyland on 17 December 2008 whilst working a Glasgow Central–Birmingham New St service.

Below Left: 221115 departs from Manchester Piccadilly on 18 April 2008 with a service to Reading.

Below Right: 221118 stands in Preston on 29 November 2007 awaiting departure with a Birmingham New St–Edinburgh service.

221120 curves through Clay Cross on 9 November 2007 with a southbound Cross Country service.

Trainsets operating with Virgin Trains livery and Cross Country branding

The temporary branding applied to the Virgin Trains livery pending a repaint into Cross Country corporate livery.

221122 stands in Manchester Piccadilly on 7 February 2008 awaiting departure with a service to Plymouth.

A 'Super Voyager' trainset curves through Portway on 26 June 2008 whilst nearing Tamworth with a southbound Cross Country service.

A 'Super Voyager' trainset curves through Portway on 26 June 2008 whilst nearing Tamworth with a southbound Cross Country service.

Right: A 'Super Voyager' trainset heads past Colton Junction on 11 March 2008 whilst working a northbound Cross Country service.

Below: 4-car 'Super Voyager' 221141 curves through Elford on 26 June 2008 shortly after leaving Tamworth with a northbound Cross Country service.

Bottom: 221119 drifts through Edinburgh's Princes St Gardens on 5 May 2008 whilst working an Aberdeen–Plymouth service.

221133 passes Elford shortly after leaving Tamworth on 2 July 2009 with a northbound Cross Country service.

221134 passes Drem on 25 August 2009 with a northbound Cross Country service.

221119 weaves into Basingstoke on 18 April 2011 with a Manchester Piccadilly–Bournemouth service.

221131 passes Portway shortly after leaving Tamworth on 28 January 2009 whilst working a northbound Cross Country service.

A 'Super Voyager' trainset curves through Longbridge on 16 May 2012 whilst working a southbound Cross Country service.

4-car 'Super Voyager' 221141 curves through Clay Cross on 3 April 2009 with a northbound Cross Country service.

Four scenes from Copmanthorpe (on the outskirts of York) during 26 October 2012.

221121 works a Plymouth–Glasgow Central service.

221131 works a Penzance–Glasgow Central service.

221136 works a Plymouth–Edinburgh service.

221139 works a Birmingham New St–Newcastle service.

Right: A 'Super Voyager' trainset passes Dalmeny on 22 August 2011 whilst working an Aberdeen–Plymouth service.

Below Left: 221136 curves through Portway on 26 November 2008 as it approaches Tamworth with a southbound Cross Country service.

Below Right: 221121 stands in Manchester Piccadilly on 19 January 2012 after arriving with a Cross Country service.

Crossing the Forth Bridge

A 'Super Voyager' trainset is viewed from South Queensferry harbour on 27 May 2012 as it crosses with a Plymouth–Aberdeen service.

Right: A 'Super Voyager' trainset approaches North Queensferry on 22 August 2009 with a Plymouth–Aberdeen service.

Below Left: A 'Super Voyager' trainset crosses from Dalmeny on 20 August 2011 with a Plymouth–Aberdeen service.

Below Right: A 'Super Voyager' trainset approaches Dalmeny on 28 May 2012 with a Dundee–Plymouth service.

Section 3:
Class 222 'Meridian'

3.1: Midland Mainline

The privatisation of British Railways in 1994 led to the first Midland Main Line franchise being awarded to National Express which began operating services under the Midland Mainline (MM) brand from April 1996 for a period of ten years. The company initially operated services with HST trainsets and ordered Class 170/1 'TurboStar' 2-car and 3-car trainsets to operate the semi fast services. In August 2000 the company was granted a 2-year extension by the Strategic Rail Authority (SRA) conditional on the ordering of new rolling stock and a commitment to operate an hourly service to Leeds.

MM elected to order seven x 9-car and sixteen x 4-car trainsets (numbered 222001–007; 222008–023 respectively) based on the 'Voyager' design but subject to modifications that mean they cannot couple up to the 'Voyager' trainsets; the new trainsets were designated 'Meridian' by MM. The order was placed in February 2002 but when deliveries began in May 2004 the SRA had revoked the proposed Leeds

hourly service and decided that the 9-car trainsets were unsuitable for use. Their use was finally allowed from July 2005 and they began operating the London–Sheffield service, supported by the 4-car trainsets operating the semi-fast services to Derby and Nottingham.

MM quickly realised that it had over-estimated its need for first class accommodation and, in order to provide more standard class accommodation, the company reduced the 9-car sets to 8-car sets and converted 222011–017 to 5-car trainsets at the end of 2006.

In September 2006 the Department for Transport (DfT), as successor to the SRA, restructured the franchises with the MM franchise being supplemented with some Central Trains services to create a new East Midlands franchise. This was awarded to Stagecoach in June 2007 and the new company began operating under the East Midlands Trains (EMT) branding from 11 November 2007.

9-car Class 222

222006 powers through Tupton on 5 July 2006 whilst working a St Pancras–Sheffield service.

9-car Class 222 222007 draws away from Loughborough on 15 August 2005 whilst working a St Pancras–Nottingham service.

Right: 222010 passes Colton Junction on 31 March 2004 whilst working a driver training run returning from York to the maintenance base at Crofton.

Below Left: 222019 passes Harrowden Junction as it approaches Wellingborough on 27 April 2007 with a southbound service to St Pancras.

Below Right: 222011 passes Tupton on 5 July 2006 whilst working a Sheffield–St Pancras service.

222013 curves into Market Harborough on 12 August 2005 whilst preparing to stop with its St Pancras–Nottingham service.

A 'Meridian' trainset curves through Clay Cross on 7 May 2005 whilst working a Sheffield–St Pancras service.

222019 passes Harrowden Junction on 27 April 2007 whilst working a southbound service to St Pancras.

222020 stands in Sheffield on 13 May 2005 after its arrival with a service from St Pancras.

De-branded in preparation for the new franchise to begin 2 days later, 222022 curves through Clay Cross on 9 November 2007 whilst running an ecs service from Sheffield to Derby.

222022 + 222015 call at Market Harborough on 12 August 2005 whilst working a Nottingham–St Pancras service.

222018 passes Harrowden Junction on 27 April 2007 whilst working a northbound service from St Pancras.

De-branded in preparation for a change of franchisee two days later, an 8-car 'Meridian' trainset curves through Clay Cross on 9 November 2007 whilst working a St Pancras–Sheffield service.

Class doyen 222001, in 8-car formation, passes Harrowden Junction on 27 April 2007 whilst working a southbound service to St Pancras.

Benefitting from the extra coach, 222014 is operating as a 5-car 'Meridian' trainset on 27 April 2007 whilst passing Harrowden Junction with a southbound service to St Pancras.

222003, in 8-car formation, passes Harrowden Junction on 27 April 2007 whilst working a northbound service from St Pancras.

222006 *City of Leicester*, in 8-car formation, passes Harrowden Junction on 27 April 2007 whilst working a northbound service from St Pancras.

3.2: East Midlands Trains

The new East Midlands franchise was awarded to Stagecoach in June 2007 and the company began operating its services as East Midlands Trains (EMT) on 11 November 2007. The new franchisee adopted the Stagecoach house livery of orange and blue on a white base; whilst retaining the Midland Mainline (MM) fleet of HSTs and 'Meridian' trainsets EMT also leased Class 156 'Sprinter' and Class 158 'Express Sprinter' trainsets to operate the additional services that were now part of the new franchise.

Between March 2008 and October 2008 EMT reconfigured the trainsets to create 6 x 7-car trainsets (222001–006) and 17 x 5-car trainsets (222007–023). The 7-car trainsets were diagrammed to operate the St Pancras - Sheffield services whilst the HST trainsets operate the St Pancras–Nottingham services and the 5-car trainsets operate the semi-fast services from St Pancras to Corby, Derby, Nottingham and Sheffield.

Bearing the livery of its previous operator, 222019 is operating as a 4-car 'Meridian' on 7 February 2008 whilst waiting to depart from St Pancras with a semi-fast service to Nottingham.

222013 races up the Midland Main Line by Cossington on 19 March 2013 whilst working a St Pancras–Nottingham semi-fast service.

222012 stands in York on 9 November 2013 whilst awaiting departure with a York–St Pancras service.

Scenes of 'Meridian' trainsets operating in 7-car formations include:

Opposite Above: Class doyen 222001 curving through Kibworth Harcourt on 9 February 2011 whilst working a Sheffield–St Pancras service.

Opposite Below: Class doyen 222001 curving through Clay Cross on 3 April 2009 whilst working a St Pancras–Sheffield service.

Right: 222005 *City of Nottingham* racing through Sutton Bonington on 14 October 2009 whilst working a Sheffield–St Pancras service.

Below Left: 222003 *Tornado* passing Cossington on 19 March 2013 whilst working a St Pancras–Sheffield service.

Below Right: 222006 *City of Leicester* curving through Kibworth Harcourt on 9 February 2011 whilst working a St Pancras–Sheffield service.

222008 passes Wyfordby on 24 July 2013 whilst working a Corby–Derby ecs service following the completion of a St Pancras–Corby service.

222023 passes Cossington on 19 March 2013 whilst working a St Pancras–Nottingham service.

Right: 222015 curves through Sutton Bonington on 14 October 2009 whilst working a St Pancras–Derby service.

Below Left: 222011 curves through Clay Cross on 3 April 2009 whilst working a St Pancras–Sheffield service.

Below Right: 222007 passes Cossington on 19 March 2013 whilst working a St Pancras–Sheffield service.

222021 passes Cossington on 19 March 2013 whilst working a St Pancras–Nottingham service.

4.1: Hull Trains

Hull Trains (HT) is an Open Access Operator owned by First Group whose 4-year agreement was confirmed in December 1999 for services to begin on 25 September 2000; further extensions have seen the current agreement (as at June 2017) operative until 2029.

The initial service was provided by the loan of Class 170/2 3-car units from sister company Anglia Railways but a change in rolling stock policy enforced by the Strategic Rail Authority (SRA) resulted in an order being placed in March 2004 for four x 4-car 'Meridian' trainsets and the loan of four Class 170/3 'TurboStar' trainsets 170393–396 until the 'Meridian' order could be delivered.

When received in May 2005, the trainsets were designated as 'Pioneer' by Hull Trains and they continued operating until 2009 when increased custom led the company to lease four spare Class 180 5-car 'Adelante' trainsets which had been released by sister company First Great Western (FGW) thus releasing the 'Pioneer' fleet for re-leasing to East Midlands Trains.

The branding and livery selected by Hull Trains for its new fleet as displayed on 222102 when (opposite) stabled at Hull for crew training on 8 June 2005.

A 'Pioneer' trainset races past Fenwick Crossing on 14 July 2006 whilst working a Hull–Kings Cross service.

Above Left: Class doyen 222101 calls at Selby on 14 June 2005 whilst working a Kings Cross–Hull service.

Above Right: A 'Pioneer' trainset races past Fenwick Crossing on 14 July 2006 whilst working a Hull–Kings Cross service.

Below Left: 222103 enters Selby on 14 June 2005 whilst working a Hull–Kings Cross service. In January 2007 this set was damaged whilst undergoing maintenance and repairs took two years to complete. During that period stock shortages were eased by the hire of Class 86/1 86101 *Sir William Stanier FRS* + stock to work supplementary Doncaster–Kings Cross services on occasion.

Below Right: 222104 awaits departure from Selby on 14 June 2005 whilst working a Hull–Kings Cross service.

The 'Pioneer' units were initially delivered without names but, shortly after being introduced to service, the name of local (to Hull) celebrities were applied although subsequently removed when the trainsets were transferred to East Midland Trains.

222103 *Sir Terry Farrar* approaches Selby on 31 May 2006 whilst working a Hull–Kings Cross service.

222104 *Dr John Godber* races past Heck on 31 May 2006 whilst working a Hull–Kings Cross service.

222104 *Dr John Godber* departs from Selby on 31 May 2006 whilst working a Kings Cross–Hull service.

222102 *Professor Stuart Parker* approaches Selby on 31 May 2006 whilst working a Hull–Kings Cross service.

222102 *Professor Stuart Parker* races past Heck Ings on 10 July 2008 whilst working a Hull–Kings Cross service.

Class doyen 222101 *Professor George Gray* races past Burn Lane on 31 May 2006 whilst working a Hull–Kings Cross service.

4.2: East Midland Trains

The decision by Hull Trains to lease spare Class 180 'Adelante' 5-car trainsets in order to meet increased passenger demand led to the availability of the 'Pioneer' trainsets which were quickly re-leased to East Midlands Trains (EMT). Initially they were obtained to provide the St Pancras to Corby service that EMT had agreed to provide as part of its franchise agreement but they were quickly subsumed into the operating fleet and, as at June 2017, are operated as 'common user' with the 5-car 'Meridian' trainsets.

Below: 222103 passes Cossington on 19 March 2013 whilst working a Nottingham–St Pancras service.

Above: Class doyen 222101 passes Cossington on 19 March 2013 whilst working a Corby–Derby ecs service after completing a St Pancras–Corby service.

Below: 222103 passes Sutton Bonington on 14 October 2009 whilst working a Derby–St Pancras service.

222102 passes Cossington on 19 March 2013 whilst working a St Pancras–Derby service.

222104 curves through Kibworth Harcourt on 9 February 2011 whilst working a St Pancras–Nottingham service.